The

THE NOBLE EXPERIMENT

The problems of alcoholism and the vicious conditions in many saloons drew numerous Americans into the prohibition movement, which by 1919 was strong enough to win national approval as the Eighteenth Amendment to the United States Constitution. This amendment, which prohibited the manufacture, transportation, or sale of intoxicating liquor, went into effect in 1920. Many Americans were still determined to drink, however; illegal drinking places sprang up in most cities. Indeed, it became glamorous and fashionable to drink, and for the first time women began to appear in bars. Because supplying alcohol was illegal, its control passed quickly into the hands of the most ruthless criminals; the money they gained from it made them rich and strong and helped them organize and develop criminal gangs. These powerful gangsters were able to bribe policemen and officials to let them operate freely. Public respect for all laws started to weaken. Many Americans began to feel that prohibition was a mistake, and that it caused more evils than it cured. This feeling grew until finally the Eighteenth Amendment was repealed in 1933, leaving behind only the criminal gangs, which by then had evolved into a nationwide organization that Americans still have with them.

PRINCIPALS

Wayne B. Wheeler (1869–1927), dedicated prohibitionist who rose to control of the Anti-Saloon League of America at a time when it was the most powerful political force in the country.

John Torrio (1882–1957), underworld leader who consolidated the small criminal groups in Chicago into one of the first modern gangs.

Herbert Hoover (1874–1964), President of the United States from 1929 to 1933. Hoover was the first President who took direct interest in prohibition enforcement. It was he who referred to the Eighteenth Amendment as "an experiment noble in motive and far-reaching in purpose."

Al Capone (1899–1947), criminal chief who took over Torrio's gang and made it into one of the most efficient and dangerous criminal groups in the country.

Franklin D. Roosevelt (1882–1945), President of the United States from 1933 to 1945. He promised to achieve repeal of the Eighteenth Amendment when he took office as President.

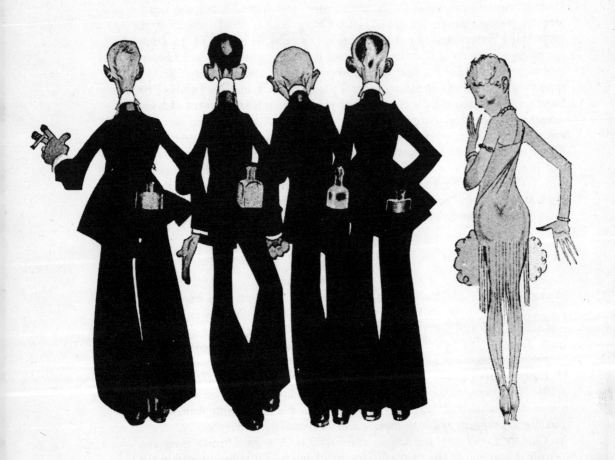

The hip flask, which made its appearance during prohibition days, became a symbol of an era that the Eighteenth Amendment had ushered in — "an experiment noble in motive and far-reaching in purpose." (New York Historical Society)

A FOCUS BOOK

The Noble Experiment,
1919–33

The Eighteenth Amendment Prohibits Liquor in America

by James P. Barry

illustrated with photographs and contemporary prints

FRANKLIN WATTS, INC.
New York
1972

The authors and publishers of the Focus Books wish to acknowledge the helpful editorial suggestions of Professor Richard B. Morris.

SBN: 531-02454-7

Contents

Famed evangelist Billy Sunday driving home a point during prohibition days. (Photo by Cushing)

The Night Before

On the evening of January 15, 1920, Billy Sunday, a well-known evangelist, held a mock funeral service in Norfolk, Virginia.

A casket 20 feet long was carried on a truck from the railroad station to Sunday's church. In it was a huge figure of John Barleycorn, the cartoon character that represented alcoholic drink. Behind the casket walked a man dressed as the Devil; he displayed great sorrow. On either side of the coffin strode mourners who wore tall black hats and black mourning bands on their arms. In the church, the "Devil" was joined by a bedraggled group costumed to look like drunkards. Throughout the service the "Devil" wept and the drunkards moaned.

The Reverend Billy in his funeral oration said of Barleycorn, "You were God's worst enemy; you were hell's best friend." And then he announced, "The reign of tears is over.... The slums will soon be only a memory. We will turn our prisons into factories and our jails into storehouses and corncribs."

The reason for this surprising forecast was simple: the next day prohibition went into effect throughout the United States, and the manufacture, sale, and transportation of intoxicating drinks was to be illegal.

That same evening in New York there was a farewell party to alcohol, given in the Park Avenue Hotel. The walls and tables of the dining room were covered in black, the napkins were black, and the glasses were black. The orchestra played funeral marches between the dances.

At the end of the party, spotlights were turned on two black-clad young couples sitting together at a black-covered table; there they poured out the final drops from black bottles, while they wept into their handkerchiefs.

In Chicago there were similar farewell parties. But also in Chicago that night six masked men took over a railroad yard, tying up and gagging the watchman and yardmaster and locking up several other railroaders. The crooks then carried away from the two boxcars a hundred thousand dollars' worth of whiskey.

The prohibition era had begun.

Drinkers enjoy a final round in a New York bar the day before prohibition goes into effect. (Brown Brothers)

An illustration from The Bottle and the Pledge, *an early temperance tale depicting the evils of drink. Scene shows how liquor ruins a happy home as husband persuades his wife to imbibe. (New York Public Library)*

The Prohibition Movement

Since colonial times there had been groups of people who thought that the drinking of alcohol was sinful, just as there were groups who thought that smoking tobacco was evil and drinking coffee was wicked. These people based their dislikes on moral principles as much as they did on medical grounds, though they did not fail to point out that the things they disliked were hazards to health. The people who felt that alcohol was bad, however, could show immediate evidence of what it did. There were enough drunkards and alcoholics around to make it plain that drinking could be an evil. Alcoholism then was as great a problem as it is today. And so the temperance movement — as the movement to prohibit alcoholic drink inaccurately called itself — gradually became stronger. It became strong enough, in fact, to bring prohibition to a number of individual states in the 1880's, but by the early 1900's most of those prohibition laws had been repealed. During this time, however, the

[3]

Cartoon shows WCTU's Carry Nation, complete with hatchet, after having broken up a neighborhood saloon. (Photo by Cushing)

prohibition movement enlisted as its allies the progressive movement (the rural liberals who blamed most social ills on big-city businesses and banks) and the women's suffrage movement.

Many women in smaller cities and in the rural areas were leaders in the prohibition movement. Of the feminine groups, the Women's Christian Temperance Union was the best known and strongest. The most famous member of the WCTU was Carry Nation, a grim-jawed woman in her fifties who lived in Kansas at the turn of the century. Kansas had a prohibition law, but it was almost universally ignored; hundreds of saloons openly sold liquor

[4]

in most parts of the state. In 1900 Carry sailed into a saloon near her home and broke up the bottles and furniture; she went on to destroy two more saloons in the same town. The results were so satisfactory that she then visited Wichita, the second largest city in Kansas, and smashed up the biggest and most prosperous saloon there. The authorities locked her up, but they had a problem; how could they charge her with destroying a saloon when legally saloons did not exist in Kansas? She was soon released.

For the next few years, Carry, and the hatchet that became her trademark, attacked more saloons, mostly in Kansas, where their illegal status gave her some immunity from arrest, but at times in other states as well. She was a religious fanatic who had visions in which she fought with the Devil and talked to God. On occasion, when the minister of her church announced that the congregation would sing a particular hymn, Carry would stand up and say firmly that they would sing another one; then she and her WCTU stalwarts would thunder it out, overriding anyone brave enough to follow the minister's lead. Several members of her family were insane; her mother had had the firm conviction that she was Queen Victoria. Carry's first husband had been a drunkard, and her second husband — with whom she lived in Kansas — was an impoverished failure. She and her daughter were estranged. She wrote, "I saw others with their loving children and husbands and I would wish their condition were mine." Modern psychiatrists could find many reasons for her holy joy in smashing the saloons, but in her day her exploits made wonderful newspaper stories, in which she was usually treated as being uproariously funny. In fact, she became a national figure, and thus in her own strange way she was able to advertise the cause of prohibition.

There were also more seriously organized campaigns to ban

alcohol. A Prohibition Party had been formed some years before to press for national prohibition as well as other reforms, such as universal suffrage and public education, but it had never been very successful. However, what was to become for a brief period the strongest political force in the United States was formed in Ohio in 1893. It was called the Anti-Saloon League, and it first sprang from the town and college of Oberlin, which had both been strong abolitionist centers at the time of the Civil War. In 1895 the Ohio league was merged into a national league, the Anti-Saloon League of America, and a major reform movement was under way. What had previously been a disorganized mass of temperance groups, each working in its own way, within a few years became a national organization led by able men and advised by clever lawyers, which turned out more than 40 tons of propaganda material each month from its own printing plant in Westerville, Ohio.

Typical of the propaganda turned out by the Anti-Saloon League was this cartoon entitled "The Full Father and the Empty Stocking." (Photo by Cushing)

The league was closely identified with rural America and with the Protestant clergy in small-town and country churches. It called itself "the church in action against the saloon." People throughout America contributed to it as regularly as they did to their own churches; often the collections were made by the churches. No doubt many of these people felt that they were contributing to a religious war.

Wisely, the Anti-Saloon League refused to identify itself with any political party, a move that seriously hurt the Prohibition Party, while giving the league itself added stature and leverage. It would support any candidate of any party who promised to do the league's bidding. Its leaders were familiar with every political trick, and they felt that in a holy war no political move could be evil, whether it be lying about an opponent, blackmailing him, or even when necessary buying his support. One agent of the league, William E. Johnson, better known as "Pussyfoot" Johnson, wrote that he had lied, bribed, and drunk in order to put over prohibition. "The lies that I have told would fill a big book," he announced proudly.

Many opponents of the Anti-Saloon League also lied, bribed, and politicked in other dishonest fashions, but generally they did it much less skillfully. The league was run by political pros, while its antagonists seem always to have been tripping over their own feet. The two sides were conveniently labeled the "drys" and the "wets." The drys were cool and clever, while the wets often mixed stupidity with arrogance. The United States Brewers' Association, for example, sent out blacklists of companies that they claimed opposed the sale of alcoholic drinks. Among them they listed hotels that observed Sunday closing laws and even the H. J. Heinz Co. because Heinz was president of a Sunday-school association that had backed prohibition. Many big companies were listed simply because they discouraged excessive drinking among their employees.

The wet forces were also divided. There were the distillers, who made whiskey and gin; there were the brewers, who made beer; and there were the vintners, who made wine. None of them trusted the others. In times of stress they were more likely to go at each other's throats than at the throats of their common enemies. On one occasion the National Liquor Dealers' Association made the

"Wettest block in the world," Kansas City, Missouri. With Kansas "dry" and Missouri "wet," this city block at the state line boasted that every building housed a saloon before prohibition went into effect. (Photo by Cushing)

fairly accurate but scarcely politic statement, "The average brewer in a mad desire for wealth is careless of public sentiment. He has no respect for law, regulation, or public decency. His business is to corrupt public officials that he may thrive. The brewers of the United States are a menace to society."

American brewers at that time financed some 80 percent of the saloons in the country through mortgages. They owned many saloons outright, leased others, and owned the fixtures in still more. If an independent saloonkeeper displeased them, the brewers could cut off his supply. About 90 percent of the alcoholic drinks sold were beer; that was where the money was in the saloon business. But there were several times more saloons than the market could legiti-

Anti-Saloon League cartoons also zeroed in on the workingman's pay envelope, which taverns outside factories would cheerfully cash. (Photo by Cushing)

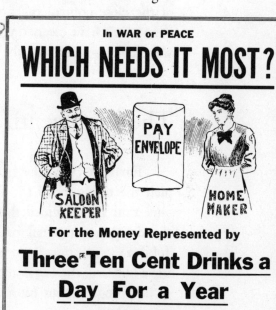

mately support; in some city areas for example, there were saloons on every corner of every intersection, plus others in the middle of the block. As a result they were forced to compete in every way possible. They ignored closing times and installed prostitutes; they served drinks to children and known alcoholics. They saved money by cutting corners — many of the places were seldom cleaned. The sawdust on the floor was a practical way of absorbing the vomit and stale beer. Much of the whiskey they sold was rotten stuff poured from good bottles. Saloons were also located just outside the gates of many factories, and were often the first places that workingmen cashed their paychecks. Of course there were also quiet, well-run saloons, but these were a small minority. Because of the close control the brewers held over the saloons, they could at any time have cleaned up the situation. But that was the way they wanted it — that way they made more money.

The Eighteenth Amendment

Early in 1913, the trustees of the Anti-Saloon League met to plan the celebrations for their twentieth-anniversary year. At the same time they decided that they were now strong enough to make the drive for national prohibition. At the league's Twenty-Year Jubilee Convention, held in Columbus, Ohio, that November during a blizzard, the keynote speaker called for nationwide prohibition to be brought about by a constitutional amendment.

"Then the convention cut loose," related one of those present, Wayne B. Wheeler. "With a roar as wild as the raging storm outside it jumped to its feet and yelled approval."

[10]

Wheeler, a lawyer who by 1913 was national attorney for the Anti-Saloon League, was destined to become its strongest leader and a virtual dictator of the prohibition movement. He had risen through the Ohio Anti-Saloon League by a combination of drive, intelligence, and skillful politics and had been for several years state superintendent of that body. A slight, short man, he had a round face with a receding hairline, wore rimless glasses and sported a moustache, and was noted for his wide — if thin-lipped — smile.

The league prepared the ground for its amendment slowly and carefully. It arranged for friendly senators and representatives to submit resolutions calling for a prohibition amendment to each house of Congress; then it let the resolutions remain in the hands of the legislative committees for a year while it worked hard in the congressional elections of 1914 to elect men who favored prohibition.

First, the league saw to it that incumbent congressmen and senators were flooded with letters, telegrams, and petitions in favor of prohibition from people in their home districts. At the same time

Wayne B. Wheeler (left), national attorney for the Anti-Saloon League and virtual dictator of the movement for prohibition, chats with Bishop James H. Darlington. (Photo by Cushing)

it sent out speakers throughout the United States to battle the wets and drum into the public's ears the need for prohibition. Initially, there were some twenty thousand of these traveling speakers, most of them volunteers; but by the end of the campaign National Superintendent P. A. Baker commanded fifty thousand volunteer and professional speakers. While this was going on, the Westerville printing plant operated on three shifts, turning out freight-car loads of propaganda. The Washington headquarters of the league directed the battle in every district. "We kept the field workers advised of

Prohibition campaign cartoons such as this flooded the nation from Wheeler's Westerville, Ohio, headquarters. This one, plugging an inherited appetite for liquor, was entitled "Putting the Mortgage on the Cradle." (Photo by Cushing)

the attitude of every individual member of Congress," Wheeler said, "and suggested ways to the local workers of winning converts."

As a result, the drys won a number of seats in Congress. They decided to try their strength, and late in 1914 pressed for the constitutional amendment that would bring prohibition. The results were a moral victory but a practical failure: the vote was 197 to 190 in favor of the amendment, but a two-thirds vote was needed to pass it and send it on to the states for ratification. In 1916 another Congress was elected and the Anti-Saloon League was in the fight hotter and harder than ever. After the election was over, they were certain that they had enough seats to win the next trial. But when that Congress first met in 1917, it had more pressing business; President Woodrow Wilson called it into a special session to declare a state of war with Germany — and the United States was in World War I.

The basic issue of permanent constitutional prohibition was almost immediately blurred by a squabble over wartime prohibition. Among the wartime measures was a food control bill. The drys inserted in it a provision that no grain or other foodstuff could be used to make beverage alcohol. The brewers and vintners promptly deserted the distillers and mustered all their political strength to bring about a compromise exempting beer and wine from the ban. They were successful, but as the war continued, President Wilson, partly because of dry pressure and partly because of wartime needs, put additional restrictions on the making of beer.

Meanwhile, the drys continued the battle with every possible argument. One of the strongest appeals was that the brewers, most of whom were of German descent, were traitors to the American cause. "The liquor traffic aids forces in our country whose loyalty is called into question at this hour," Wayne Wheeler contended.

[13]

The prohibition campaign also cashed in on the fact that most brewers were of German descent. Here, in a cartoon titled "Two Birds — One Stone," an outraged U.S. taxpayer tries to knock off both the Kaiser and an American brewer with a "prohibition" stone during World War I. (Photo by Cushing)

"The liquor traffic is the strong financial supporter of the German-American Alliance. . . . Its leaders urge its members to vote only for those who stand for Germanism and oppose prohibition." Thus a vote against prohibition was made to seem a vote for treason.

At the same time that this was going on, the drys pushed forward with their plan for a constitutional amendment. In June of 1917 a senatorial committee favorably reported on a resolution to add the Eighteenth Amendment to the Constitution of the United States. In late July and early August it was debated briefly in the Senate, and was then adopted by that body in a vote of 65 to 20.

The Eighteenth Amendment came before the House of Representatives in mid-December of 1917. The House spent one day in debate over it, then adopted it by 282 votes to 128. Next the amendment had to be ratified by the states. In passing it, the Congress had specified that it must be ratified within seven years; many wets foolishly thought that this could never happen. But the state legislatures were exactly where the Anti-Saloon League had its greatest strength; it knew how to pull the political strings there even better than on the national level. State after state hastened to ratify. In January of 1919 Nebraska became the thirty-sixth state to do so; the necessary three-quarters of the states had approved the amendment in slightly over one year. Even the drys were amazed. Eventually all but two states, Connecticut and Rhode Island, ratified the amendment, which forbade the manufacture, sale, or transportation of intoxicating liquors in the United States, or the importation of them.

One year after it was ratified, the Eighteenth Amendment went into effect. In order to provide for enforcement, Congress passed the National Prohibition Act on October 28, 1919. It was commonly known as the Volstead Act because it was sponsored by Andrew J. Volstead, a Minnesota congressman. But it was actually written by none other than Wayne B. Wheeler. Wheeler must have been weary after his victory, for instead of his usual efficient product he turned out a long, rambling, and sometimes vague document that would give rise to legal arguments for some years to come.

Andrew J. Volstead, a Minnesota congressman, sponsored the National Prohibition Act. (Photo by Cushing)

To the surprise of everyone concerned, President Wilson vetoed the act and sent it back to Congress. He explained that the lumpy bill contained not only provisions for enforcing the Eighteenth Amendment, but also provisions for enforcing wartime prohibition in a war that had been over for a year, and he objected to such a sloppy procedure. Congress immediately overrode the veto, and the Volstead Act became law.

The Speakeasies

On January 17, 1920, prohibition agents arrested twelve liquor-law violators in New York, but it took a little longer for them to go into action in other cities. It was two weeks after prohibition became law before agents instigated the first raid on a Chicago "speakeasy" (the term had already been in the English language for some time to denote a place where alcoholic drink was sold illegally). At Clark and Kinzie streets, an establishment called the Red Lantern had been set up in a basement. There the federal agents closed in, rounded up forty well-dressed men and women, and took them off to jail. As one local newspaper commented, "Nothing like this had happened before."

But occasional raids would not keep determined drinkers from visiting speakeasies or enterprising businessmen from running them. Soon there were almost as many different kinds of speakeasies as there were types of customers. In the dives along the Bowery in New York, the bums bought "smoke," a poisonous wood alcohol that had been strained through newspapers in the belief that this somehow purified it. Farther uptown, Yale and Harvard graduates

Left, cartoonist Rollin Kirby's blue-nosed tyrant pictured here became almost a symbol of the spirit of prohibition in America. (New York Public Library) Below, a typical speakeasy in New York City during prohibition days. (Photo by Cushing)

patronized speakeasies that were like pleasant clubs, which sold liquor that even tasted a little like the real thing. There were other speakeasies that attracted the intellectuals of the day, such as the poet Dorothy Parker and the newspaper writer Heywood Broun, as well as other clubs that catered to men interested in sports. There was the Artists' and Writers' Club, patronized heavily by newspapermen. The most unusual speakeasy, however, was the Bridge Whist Club, which was open at all hours, provided excellent drinks and good food, and had the pleasant atmosphere of a truly well-run saloon; it was owned and operated by the Prohibition Bureau of the United States government.

The excuse for this fantastic venture was that the Bridge Whist Club supposedly trapped bootleggers. One of the back booths was equipped with a hidden microphone. Bootleggers were to be led to this booth, plied with good drink, and then questioned about their own sources. Meanwhile, someone in the back room would listen in and write it all down. This procedure actually did work a few times, but on at least one occasion it backfired. One bootlegger, realizing what was happening, described in much detail the personal lives of several notable drys who were his customers, among them a few leaders of the Anti-Saloon League, and explained just what they drank, and how. Needless to say, this evidence was never used.

The Prohibition Bureau was, in fact, the most despised agency of the United States government. It was placed under the Treasury Department, which did not want it, rather than under the Justice Department, which might have administered it with some efficiency. The Commissioner of Internal Revenue, who was to supervise it, had pointed out that he was already overburdened and could not take on this extra job, but the Volstead Act gave it to him anyway. Then Wayne Wheeler helpfully volunteered to assist him; it was

Wheeler who organized and staffed the bureau. Through this maneuver the dry army was controlled by the Anti-Saloon League. Personnel of the bureau were exempt from Civil Service requirements, and as a result it was filled with political appointments, all of whom had to have Wheeler's approval. Prohibition agents were not well paid, and until nearly the end of prohibition they received no training. Understandably, their work often was poor. The honest agents soon decided that there was no point in working long hours under dangerous conditions for little pay, and they left the bureau. The dishonest ones quickly found that their jobs offered tremendous opportunities for graft. Thus the bureau attracted and retained exactly the wrong men.

But there were two of the honest agents who worked very hard, and because they were natural clowns they received a great deal of publicity. The nature of the publicity, however, did not contribute to the dignity of law enforcement. These men were Izzy Einstein and Moe Smith, whose homes were on the Lower East Side

Two hardworking prohibition agents were Izzy Einstein (left) and Moe Smith, shown here decked out in outlandish disguises and off to raid a speakeasy. (New York Public Library)

of New York. Izzy was 5 feet tall and Moe was 5 feet 2, but each of them weighed more than 200 pounds, most of it in muscle. They seldom had to carry guns. Izzy, an accomplished actor, seems to have been able to hypnotize his victims into believing that he was someone completely different. At various times he pretended to be a violinist, a college boy, or a lawyer, and people always believed him. Izzy and Moe wore fantastic disguises, claiming to be gravediggers or football players, and the saloonkeepers and bootleggers accepted them at face value. Once, when the guard at the peephole in a speakeasy door asked Izzy who he was, the genial Einstein replied that he was a prohibiton agent. The guard, laughing, opened the door and let him in.

Other agents were much more willing to carry guns than were Izzy and Moe, but their lack of training and discipline made them dangerous. Innocent citizens were wounded and sometimes killed. The agents involved were seldom convicted of any crime. Most other law-enforcement bodies wanted as little contact as possible

Federal prohibition agents are shown here after a successful raid in the mid-1920's. (Perry Pictures)

with the prohibition agents, whom they looked upon with contempt, and as a result would not share information with them; they also felt, with some reason, that information given to the graft-ridden bureau would probably go right back to the bootleggers. Many state and city police agencies refused to enforce the prohibition law at all. The Volstead Act had specified that the states would have "concurrent" power to enforce the prohibition law, and according to the drys this meant that they had to do it — but according to a number of the states themselves it meant that they did not have to do it unless they wanted to. There was no way the federal government could force them to undertake the costly and unpleasant job.

The prohibition law quickly closed down all the good New York restaurants, which had attempted to go on serving alcoholic drinks and had been summarily padlocked by the prohibition agents. One result was that anyone who wanted to go to a restaurant almost automatically found himself going to a speakeasy. Nightclubs also boomed, and the famous nightclub entertainer Texas Guinan, who always addressed her patrons, "Hello, sucker," would ask, "Where the hell would I be without prohibition?" The answer, of course, was nowhere. The same thing could be said twice over of Larry Fay, the racketeer owner of the clubs in which Texas got her start.

"Hello, sucker!" was the usual greeting given by nightclub entertainer "Texas" Guinan to customers who were thirsty — and who didn't mind too much if the speakeasies overcharged them for their drinks. (Photo by Cushing)

As speakeasies proliferated, women began to frequent them in larger numbers. Here a young couple, in a scene taken from a movie still of the late 1920's, sample the pleasures of a cellar gin mill. (Photo by Cushing)

One of the strangest results of prohibition was that it brought women into bars. When drinking had been legal, a woman of any reputation seldom would go into a saloon. Women of the middle classes usually drank nothing alcoholic (except some of the patent medicines of the day, which were respectable even though they contained as much as 50 percent alcohol) and often joined the WCTU. Women of more affluent families drank openly in restaurants and at home; women of the working classes accepted beer and wine as normal things in life. But none of them patronized saloons. As soon as the speakeasies began to mushroom, however, women began to go to them. It had become the fashionable thing to do. Heywood Broun growled that the old saloons may have been bad, but at least in them a man didn't have to fight his way to the bar through crowds of schoolgirls.

Speakeasies flourished throughout most of the country, although in a few places there was genuine dry sentiment and in some, where other arms of the government such as the Customs Bureau held jurisdiction, the law was enforced more efficiently. But even deep in the heart of dry Texas the openly run saloons of Galveston caused one law officer to say wryly that the city was "outside the United States." By that standard, so were most of the others.

Rumrunners and Alcohol Cookers

The alcohol that was sold illegally to thirsty Americans either had to be smuggled into the United States or made there. Most of the smuggling was by water along the coasts or across the Great Lakes. Smugglers who operated over water came generally to be known as rumrunners, although rum was only a small part of the liquor they brought in.

Rumrunners used everything from fishing schooners to seaplanes to carry their wet cargoes. One of the first of these adventurers was Captain William McCoy, a tall, powerfully built merchant-marine officer who discovered this special kind of seafaring that could make a sailor rich. He was an honest man in his way, and he refused to water down the liquor he brought in or to mix it with the chemicals often used to cut smuggled alcohol. As a result, good imported whiskey was described as "the real McCoy."

But rum-running soon became something quite different from a gentlemanly game with the Coast Guard. It was illegal, and the men in it had no legal protection from other, more experienced, criminals. When rumrunners delivered their cargoes, their supposed customers might instead come aboard and take the liquor by force, beating up or killing the crew. Complete strangers might hijack the cargoes. If a Coast Guardsman or Customs inspector got in the way, the hoodlums would not hesitate to kill him. The Coast Guardsmen in turn developed nervous trigger fingers. Rum-running developed into a deadly business.

Within the United States some breweries remained open, making legal near beer, a kind of beer from which the alcohol was

The contraband rumrunner Mary Langdon, *flanked by the Coast Guard cutter* Redwing *and a small patrol boat, was seized in June, 1925. (U.S. Coast Guard Photo)*

Gangland leader Johnny Torrio, as he appeared in later years. (Photo by Cushing)

removed. Much of this drink was delivered to speakeasies where it was "needled" by a hypodermic syringe full of alcohol, kept handy by the bartender. Sometimes the syringe was filled with poisonous wood alcohol, and often serious illness was the result. The production of "cereal beverages," as the Volstead Act called near beer, was legal, so there was no problem in obtaining the raw materials; there were a good many breweries that simply turned out beer, just as it had always been made, and neglected to take out the alcohol. At the beginning, such an operation needed someone who knew a great deal about the difficult art of brewing. Most brewers did not want to go into the illegal business, but enough were willing so that it got well started.

In Chicago, for example, Joseph Stenson, a preprohibition brewer, went into partnership with a somewhat less respectable businessman, John Torrio, who had been successful in gambling and prostitution. Stenson raised money, bought breweries that had been closed down, and even installed boards of directors in the breweries — men who would, if necessary, go to jail without implicating him. Torrio provided guards for the breweries and sold and delivered the product, when necessary eliminating competition by beatings or murders. This partnership is estimated to have made $50 million in four years. When one brewery was raided in 1924, however, the situation was not so pleasant; Stenson and some of the other brewers escaped trial, although Torrio and a few of his men were convicted and sentenced. But Torrio's arrest precipitated a gang war, and the brewers, considerably shaken by all this, withdrew from the business and left it to the mobsters.

Whiskey and grain alcohol could still be made legally for medical use and for export. The number of people who needed to use alcohol as a medicine began to soar. Medical doctors of questionable ethics regularly sold prescriptions for whiskey. Later, the government set a limit on the amount of alcohol that could be prescribed. The doctors pointed out indignantly that there were quite legitimate cases in which patients needed more than that limit, but it made no difference; the drys would rather shut off the illegal flow of alcohol than worry about a few medical patients who died for lack of it. In actuality, probably few of those patients did die, at least for that reason. There was still plenty of alcohol around. Unethical druggists had an even better racket than unethical doctors, for their supply was nearly unlimited; many druggists were dispensers of illegal joy. In addition, a good deal of the alcohol supposedly intended for medical use or export was diverted into illegal channels as soon as it left the factory or warehouse; one of the richest bootleggers, George Remus of Cincinnati and St. Louis, made his fortune by such diversions. Much of what was exported went to Canada or other nearby areas and then was promptly smuggled back into the United States.

So lucrative did bootlegging liquor become that it inspired this cartoon in Life *for August, 1922. Caption read: "Summer Shack of a Struggling Young Bootlegger."*

Another source of alcohol was the moonshiner's still. Before prohibition there had been some moonshining, mainly in rural areas, in order to escape the taxes that were being levied on the regular distillers. Now a good many newcomers took up moonshining; not all of them knew what they were doing, and as a result some of the whiskey they made was highly poisonous. Moonshining also moved into the cities. Operators such as the six Genna brothers of Chicago spread portable stills through the kitchens of hundreds of tenements. The alcohol produced by the "alky cookers," as the people who

A moonshiner in the Georgia hills guarding his still. (Photo by Cushing)

tended the stills were known, was collected weekly and taken to a central warehouse where it was diluted, flavored, colored, and put in bottles that were labeled as whiskey or gin.

Industrial alcohol was still another source of bootleg drink. The Volstead Act exempted industrial alcohol from its provisions, for there were many necessary uses for it in manufacturing. The Prohibition Bureau insisted that industrial alcohol must be "denatured," which meant that something had to be added to it that made it unfit to drink. Some of the additives, such things as liquid soap, were harmless enough, but others were poisonous, even to such an extreme as sulfuric acid. Inevitably, a good deal of industrial

[28]

Above, federal agents pose with captured equipment in an underground distillery in Detroit. Below, in New York City, agents rip up a counter to see if liquor is hidden beneath it. (Photos by Cushing)

alcohol found its way into the hands of bootleggers, who made more or less successful efforts to strain out the additives. A trained chemist with a well-equipped laboratory could remove almost any of them, but most bootleggers were not trained chemists, did not have laboratories, and really didn't care. As a result, the poisons that went into industrial alcohol were estimated to have killed about forty out of every million people in the United States during one year of prohibition. In the face of newspaper protests at the virulence of the poisons being used, Wayne Wheeler made the unfortunate comment that

The "hardware of hooch." County deputies in Seattle raided this hardware supply store and confiscated copper tubing and cookers, used to manufacture illegal stills. (Photo by Cushing)

people who drank industrial alcohol were deliberate suicides. A public that remembered how the drys once accused distillers of poisoning their customers by selling them good whiskey now had to adjust to the idea of the drys putting real poison into alcohol that they knew some Americans would drink.

Above all, as prohibition went on, more and more people made alcoholic drinks in their own homes. They might be wine or beer, the latter popularly known as home brew. All of the equipment to make these drinks, and all of the ingredients, were sold openly in stores. There usually was provided a complete set of instructions, at the top of which was printed a solemn warning that under no circumstances should the following actions, which would produce an alcoholic drink in violation of the law, be undertaken by the purchaser. Other drinkers preferred raw alcohol, which was bought from druggists or bootleggers and then mixed at home with various flavorings. The easiest thing to do with it was to add glycerin and oil of juniper; the result was "bathtub gin." It was horrible stuff, but it was a good deal better than most of the concoctions that could be purchased already mixed.

The Gangs

Prohibition gave those criminals who had any sort of organization a new and wonderful opportunity. Here was a law that most of the country was apparently determined to violate. There was an immense amount of money to be made in bootlegging. There was a tremendous demand for drink and the drinkers looked upon bootleggers as public servants, even though by law they were criminals.

A citizen who would denounce a bank robber was often sympathetic to a bootlegger and would help him dodge the police. No wonder the crooks liked it; they grew rich and were, in effect, helped by their own victims.

In every big city there developed cutthroat competition for bootlegging profits. In New York such men as Frank Costello and Owney Madden began to fight their way to the top; in Philadelphia it was Maxie Hoff; in Detroit, Chester LaMare; in Kansas City, Solly Weissman. In Chicago, crime had always been a little larger than life-size, and in Chicago there emerged the biggest mobster of them all, Al Capone. The history of prohibition crime in Chicago followed the same pattern that it did in other cities, but in Chicago it was more open and frequently gaudier, and in Chicago the criminals attained more direct power.

It began when John Torrio took over the prostitution ring of Big Jim Colosimo, who was Torrio's employer. In May of 1920 Colosimo was shot in the back of the head by a gunman who, through no coincidence, had been a close associate of Torrio's a few years before in New York. Torrio paid for the ornate funeral at which the honorary pallbearers included three judges, an assistant state's attorney, a member of Congress, a state representative, and nine aldermen. Torrio then picked up the reins of Colosimo's enterprise. One of his first moves was to import from New York an up-and-coming young fellow who had been working in a dive as a dishwasher, substitute bartender, and occasional murderer. His name was Alphonse Capone.

Torrio was a master organizer. He looked out over the city of Chicago and saw a number of small criminals wallowing in the money that prohibiton had brought them. All of them were competing, sometimes violently; there was no coordination. Torrio's first move was to ensure a good supply of beer, Chicago's favorite drink. This was accomplished by going into partnership with Joseph Stenson, the preprohibition brewer turned master bootlegger. Once Torrio was able to supply a steady flow of beer, he called together the various small criminal chiefs, and pointed out to them that competition was foolish. They should divide the city into areas, he said, and each gang should operate in its own district. Dion O'Banion, an expert at bank holdups, was given the North Side. The six Genna brothers got part of the West Side. Other crooks got other sections. Torrio naturally kept a few choice areas for himself, including one South Side district that he put under the supervision of Al Capone.

In the course of slicing up the city, Torrio overlooked the four O'Donnell brothers. Spike O'Donnell, the most able of the four, was serving a term for bank robbery and the remaining three brothers were loafing along, supporting themselves by petty thuggery while waiting for Spike to be released. Then the governor of Illinois received a petition to pardon Spike; it was signed by a judge, six state senators, and five state representatives. The pleas of all these distinguished men convinced the governor, and he turned O'Donnell loose. Early in 1923 Spike returned to Chicago, got his brothers together, and set to work to carve out a piece of the city for himself. He sold better beer than Torrio, with less water in it. Torrio responded by cutting prices.

On the night of September 7, 1923, a group of O'Donnell gangsters went out to sell their products to reluctant speakeasy owners, beating up those who stubbornly insisted on dealing with Torrio. After their rounds they stopped at Klepka's speakeasy on South Lincoln Street for some light refreshment. A little later a group of Torrio's gunmen led by Frank McErline and Daniel McFall (who also happened to be a sheriff's deputy) burst in on them. McFall

Above, North Side boss Dion O'Banion. (UPI Photo) Right, "Spike" O'Donnell. (Chicago Daily News)

shouted to stick up their hands and fired a warning shot. The lights went out and the O'Donnell men scattered. One of them, a paroled lifer, named O'Connor was pushed out into the street by McFall, where another man, probably McErline, blew his head off with a shotgun blast.

Torrio evidently wanted to make his point very clear. Ten days later two of the other O'Donnell toughs who had taken part that night in the hard sell of the saloonkeepers were going somewhere in a roadster. They stopped at a main intersection and a long green touring car pulled alongside. The heavy reports of shotguns and pistols blasted in the air and the touring car moved away, leaving two dead men in the roadster.

Mayor William E. Dever, outraged, suspended the police captain in charge of the district where the murders had taken place, revoked the licenses of two thousand "soft drink" parlors that were actually speakeasies, and called in his chief of police and chief of detectives to tell them he was assuming direct control of the investigation. The legal machinery went into action. Capone was questioned without result. Torrio had left town — to attend a wake, his lawyer explained. Eventually Torrio returned and was also questioned, inconclusively. McFall, indicted for the murder of O'Connor, was tried, and acquitted.

Before McFall was brought to trial there was another skirmish. Two O'Donnell men, bringing in a truckload of beer from Joliet in December, 1923, were met by a gang of Torrio men led by McErline. They were invited into McErline's car and driven away; the next day they were discovered in a ditch with their hands tied behind them and a good deal of buckshot in them; one was dead, the other seriously wounded. McErline was arrested, then released. Early in 1924 the driver of another O'Donnell beer truck was gunned down at the wheel. Then Walter O'Donnell and an imported New York gunman were trapped in a suburban roadhouse and shot to death. Spike O'Donnell himself had by this time been attacked on ten different occasions; now with seven of his men dead, he gave up and left town.

At the same time Torrio was moving into Cicero, a suburb of Chicago. He put Capone in charge, and in short order Al became ruler of the town. In 1924 the reelection of Cicero Mayor Joseph Z. Klenha seemed doubtful. But Capone moved in two hundred thugs from Chicago; they patrolled the streets and guarded the polls, threatening citizens and slugging or kidnapping election workers and voters. Before election day ended there were five deaths and an untold number of injuries. Capone himself exchanged shots with some Chicago policemen brought in, in a futile attempt to keep order. Not surprisingly, Klenha won.

Torrio was now at the height of his career. He and Capone were raking in $30 million a year from bootlegging and about half

[35]

Gangland czar Al Capone. "Everybody calls me a racketeer," he once said. "I call myself a businessman. When I sell liquor, it's bootlegging. When my patrons serve it on a silver tray on Lake Shore Drive, it's hospitality." (Photo by Cushing)

that sum in addition from such other enterprises as gambling and prostitution. When an especially valuable shipment of booze came into Chicago, policemen were detailed to protect it. There were periodic raids on Torrio's less desirable holdings by prohibition agents, but everyone involved knew about it in advance. The important people were never there, and the ones who were raided went through the motions, knowing that they probably would never be arrested and locked up. Torrio once said, straightforwardly and without bragging, "I own the police." With a few exceptions, this was true.

But Dion O'Banion, the North Side gangster, began to undermine Torrio. O'Banion had helped the Torrio-Capone combine take over Cicero, and in return had been given part of the town. He had also induced fifty Chicago speakeasy owners to move into his section of Cicero, thus boosting his profits tremendously. Naturally, the saloons that had moved no longer bought their supplies from their former gangster sources, and thus the crooks they had left behind were unhappy. At the same time O'Banion's operations in Cicero competed more and more sharply with Torrio and Capone. In this way, ill will grew on all sides.

O'Banion was not just a troublemaker, however. He could on occasion show considerable generalship. At about this time, his men carted a million dollars' worth of bonded whiskey out of a Chicago warehouse, leaving neatly behind them an equal number of barrels of plain water. O'Banion and various police and warehouse officials were implicated but never convicted. This stroke, however, did nothing to soften the growing jealousy of other gangsters.

Then came the business of the Sieben Brewery. It was owned by Torrio, Capone, and O'Banion, plus of course Joseph Stenson behind the scenes. O'Banion took care of the deliveries. It had been operating at full capacity for three years; the federal agents finally decided that they had to do something about it and scheduled a raid for the morning of May 19. This word was passed along to O'Banion. Thereupon he went to Torrio and Capone to say that he wanted to get out of the business and retire; that he felt the enmity of the other gangs, which had been building up, was becoming too dangerous, and he wanted to sell his share in the brewery to his partners. Torrio and the others listened to his story with happy amazement; it seemed that they could now get rid of their major problem in the easiest possible way. They were pleased to accept the price of $500,000 — and the deal was closed. O'Banion said that he would turn over his papers and explain the delivery details to them at the brewery on May 19.

When the police moved in that morning they found not only plenty of beer, but also Torrio, O'Banion, and a number of their henchmen. From O'Banion's point of view it was a wonderful joke. He would probably get off with a fine; but Torrio, who had been fined the preceding year, was now a second offender and would no doubt be jailed.

O'Banion lived dangerously. In addition to his betrayal of Torrio, he had recently said: "To hell with them Sicilians" — and this had been widely quoted. As it turned out, he himself reached that "place" first. O'Banion, in a strange twist of character, also ran a florist shop as a sideline. Just before noon on November 10, three men walked into the shop. O'Banion, smiling, went toward them with an outstretched hand. One of the men, grasping his hand, pulled him off-balance and the others shot him five times; then, as he lay on the floor, someone finished him off with a sixth bullet in the head.

Who killed him? Surely Torrio had reason, and in what might have been an intentionally bizarre gesture, he had ordered $10,000 worth of flowers from O'Banion's shop the day before for the funeral of another colleague who had died a natural death. Yet, O'Banion had also been feuding with the Genna brothers, who were Sicilians and would, of course, take an extremely dark view of his often-quoted remark. It was generally thought that Mike Genna was the man who had grasped O'Banion's hand. Almost certainly the other killers were two Sicilians who had done frequent jobs for Torrio.

At any rate, O'Banion's coffin cost $10,000 and was sent by express from Philadelphia. Its walls were double, of solid silver and bronze, and its top was plate glass. Twenty-six carloads of flowers preceded the hearse; among them was a basket of roses inscribed, simply, "from Al." The burial was not in consecrated ground — the Catholic Church would not permit that — but there were three bands to lead the procession to the cemetery and five judges and numerous aldermen and legislators among the mourners. There were also Torrio and Capone and all of O'Banion's men. The police had a special detachment that moved among the gangsters present and asked them to keep the peace, at least on this day, and city officials requested that all guns be put in the care of friends until after the ceremony.

Immediately after the graveside rites, Torrio left town on an extended trip. He returned to Chicago in mid-January of 1925; late that month, as he crossed the sidewalk in front of his home, two O'Banion men came from behind a parked car and shot him five times. By February 9 he had recovered sufficiently to appear in court and receive the sentence that O'Banion had brought upon him: a $5,000 fine and nine months in prison. He was released in the fall of 1925 and a bodyguard escorted him to New York, where he sailed for Italy. He later returned to the United States, but never again to Chicago.

Gang Warfare

Capone inherited Torrio's empire. He faced the former O'Banion gang, now led by Hymie Weiss. There was open warfare between the two sides. In the spring of 1925 Angelo Genna, president of Chicago's Unione Siciliana and one of the six brothers allied with Capone, was driving through Chicago in his new, expensive roadster. A large black touring car came up behind him; in it were

Weiss and two of his men. As the touring car came abreast of the roadster, each of the gangsters in it fired a sawed-off shotgun into Genna. He died immediately. There was another funeral, similar to that for O'Banion.

The remaining Genna brothers patrolled Chicago looking for the murderers. On June 13 a group of hoodlums led by Mike Genna had a running battle with some of the Weiss gang, who got away. Mike Genna's car, in which he and three of his gangsters rode, continued to roar about the streets looking for the Weiss car. In their reckless searching they nearly collided with another auto driven by an innocent citizen. A police car was nearby and the four detectives in it saw what happened; they set out in pursuit. The gangster car stayed ahead of them, traveling through city traffic over slippery streets at 70 miles per hour. Then a truck pulled in front of Genna. His car spun twice, knocked down a lamppost, and finally halted. The police car skidded to a stop beside it as the gangsters got out on the far side. None of the policemen drew their guns. Detective Michael J. Conway walked over to the gangster car, saying "What's the idea?" to its occupants. The gangsters opened up with repeating shotguns. Three policemen fell, two of them mortally injured.

The fourth policeman, Detective William Sweeney, escaped injury. As the murderers fled he ran after them. Genna trailed at the end of the group; half a block away he turned and fired at Sweeney — or so he intended. The shotgun clicked on an empty chamber. Sweeney's pistol shot hit Genna in the leg. Trying to get away, Genna smashed in a basement window and dived through. Sweeney, accompanied by two other police officers who had arrived, shoved into the basement. Genna got off one harmless shot before they overpowered him. As he lay weak from loss of blood, an

[41]

The funeral of Angelo Genna, one of the notorious Genna brothers, was a model of gangland elegance.

Hymie Weiss, who became leader of the O'Banion gang. (UPI Photo)

ambulance arrived. Cursing, Genna kicked the stretcher-bearer in the face, and then died.

Shortly after Mike Genna's end, Sam Amatuna, who had taken over the presidency of the Unione Siciliana, was shot in the head from behind while sitting in a barber chair. One of his close allies, Eddie Zion, was shot on his way home from Amatuna's funeral, and another associate, Bummy Goldstein, was killed by a shotgun blast two weeks later. The Weiss gang was evening the score.

Meanwhile, the two gunmen who had been with Mike Genna were arrested for the murder of the two policemen. Immediately there was a drive among the Sicilians to raise money for their defense. A brother-in-law of the dead Angelo Genna donated $10,000, but refused to pay more; in the ensuing argument with the collector he was shot dead. Two wholesale grocers in the Sicilian community contributed $2,000 each, but they gave no more and openly said that the murder of Genna's brother-in-law was a disgrace. Both were shot. A wine dealer, asked for his third contribution, refused and was

[42]

shot. These four men had some stature and their murders shocked their neighborhood. They also had friends. In rapid succession four of the collectors for the fund were killed.

The two arrested Genna gunmen were tried two years later, after a tremendous amount of legal maneuvering. Their battle with the police had taken place in a busy city street, but witnesses were scarce and those who had come forth now began to lose their memories. At the end of the trial, the pair was found guilty of manslaughter of one policeman. They were then tried for the murder of the other and found not guilty. In May of 1926 they were sent to Joliet prison to serve fourteen-year terms for manslaughter; in December the Illinois Supreme Court granted them a new trial. At the end of the trial they were acquitted. They had, that court said, only resisted "unwarranted police aggression."

Capone had welcomed the gradual weakening of the Genna family, even though they nominally were his allies; they were prickly and difficult men, and they were leaders of the Sicilian community that Capone himself would have liked to control (the Sicilians ran the "alky-cooking" syndicate). With two of the Gennas and several of their henchmen dead, Al felt able to move on his own. Tony Genna received a call from a supposed friend to meet him at the corner of Grand Avenue and Curtis Street on July 8, 1925, at 6:00 P.M., to receive important information. He met the friend, they shook hands, and the other gangster held him firmly at arm's length while two gunmen appeared from nearby doors and shot him repeatedly in the back. The three remaining Genna brothers got the message; they abandoned their rackets and left town. Capone had scored a victory.

At the same time all this was going on, dozens of other gangsters were murdered all over Chicago. The reasons were often obscure.

[43]

Movie still of prohibition era depicts a typical gangland fight. Mobsters depended on fast automobiles for quick strikes and getaways. (Photo by Cushing)

The peace that Torrio had imposed was gone and old grudges now came to the surface. Carefully and cleverly Al Capone picked his way through the turmoil, allying himself with some groups and eliminating others. Three attacks were made on his own car, the slugs tearing his clothing each time but not hitting him.

The gangsters always were eager for the most modern tools. They had adopted the automobile, which at that time was just emerging as a fast and dependable piece of equipment. They learned to move quickly, strike, and speed away; in fact, they had more mobility than a good many armies of the day. They also accepted with joy the Thompson submachine gun, which supposedly was

[44]

available only to military and police forces, but which somehow became a standard weapon of the hoodlums. It was a short, heavy gun that fired the same ammunition as a .45-caliber pistol but used 50-round or 100-round magazines and spat out 150 shots per minute. Known as the tommy gun, it first achieved substantial notoriety when one was used to murder William H. McSwiggin, a twenty-six-year-old assistant state's attorney, on the night of April 27, 1926.

McSwiggin and four others, three of them known criminals and the fourth a former policeman in the pay of one of the crooks, pulled up in front of a saloon in Cicero in a Lincoln sedan belonging to one of McSwiggin's companions. As they got out, another car drove past, and someone in it with a machine gun cut loose at them. McSwiggin and two gangsters were killed; the other two men dropped to the ground quickly and escaped injury. At first the word went out from McSwiggin's office that he had been investigating crime and had been killed in line of duty. Inevitably, Capone was accused. He answered, with apparent sincerity, "Of course I didn't kill him. Why should I? I liked the kid. . . . I paid McSwiggin and I paid him plenty, and I got what I was paying for." At one point McSwiggin's father, a police sergeant, met Capone and accused him of the murder. Capone pulled out his pistol, offered it to the older man, and said, "If you think I did it, shoot me." The elder McSwiggin turned away in tears.

During the investigation of this murder, it became clear that the younger McSwiggin was probably not on an innocent investigation when he was killed. It also became evident that gangsters, politicians, and police were all interconnected. The only specific findings, however, were those of a grand jury, which blamed the gang war on the profits to be made from the illegal traffic in beer and alcohol, the ready availability of weapons, and the "widespread violation of the Volstead Act." None of these were exactly new ideas.

Capone now set out to subdue Hymie Weiss, his chief opponent. In August, Weiss and a companion, Vincent Drucci, were walking along Michigan Avenue at 10:00 A.M., threading their way through heavy foot traffic. Just as they were about to cross Ninth Street, a car pulled in toward them and three men leaned out, each firing two pistols. As Weiss, unhurt, dropped to the pavement, Drucci lunged behind a mailbox and began to return the fire. Something like thirty shots were exchanged; the only person hurt was an innocent man who was wounded in the thigh. A week later Weiss and two others were driving down Michigan Avenue when another car forced them into the curb and opened fire. Once again they got away unhurt. Capone then arranged for a peace talk with Weiss. Hymie's first demand was that the gunmen who attacked him had to be killed. The peace talk broke up.

Now it was Weiss's move. On September 20, at 1:15 P.M., Al Capone was finishing lunch at his headquarters, the Hawthorne Restaurant, in Cicero. A black touring car, equipped like a police car with a gong on the running board, came past at high speed with the gong ringing and a man beside the driver firing a tommy gun. As this decoy car disappeared, everyone in the restaurant began to rush into the street. Capone attempted to follow the same impulse, but his quick-thinking bodyguard, Frank Rio, grabbed him and tumbled him under a table.

At that moment ten cars, moving slowly at 10-foot intervals, pulled up in front of the restaurant. As each one arrived and halted, the men in it opened fire with submachine guns, pouring their shots into the building. Then from car number nine a man carrying a tommy gun walked up to the restaurant door and swept the place with a ten-second burst of bullets, while men from the tenth car guarded him with sawed-off shotguns. Then they walked back to their cars, a horn signaled, and the convoy drove off.

The most surprising part of the whole episode was that not one person was killed. The only serious casualty was a young woman sitting in a nearby parked car whose eye was struck by flying glass. Capone paid for her extensive medical care. He also paid the nearby shopkeepers for the considerable damage caused during the attack.

In addition, Capone decided that Weiss definitely had to be finished off. On October 11 Hymie left a Chicago courtroom where he had been observing the murder trial of two of his men. About 4:00 P.M. he arrived at his command post in O'Banion's old florist shop. As he and four others got out and started toward the shop, a submachine gun began to hammer in an upstairs window next door. Weiss and another man dropped dead. The remaining three were seriously injured.

On October 20 Capone called together the leaders of all the other groups, including Vincent Drucci, who had stepped up into Weiss's place. Once again the key mobsters divided up the city into zones, this time with the clear understanding that Capone was the number one boss. There was no question now about that.

The Lawless Americans

Gangsters also operated in other parts of the country. They were neither as open nor as flamboyant as the Chicagoans, and so they did not get as many newspaper headlines and their activities are harder to trace. But in Cleveland, for example, there were thirty-eight gangster murders over a five-year period, so many of them at one intersection, 110th Street and Woodland Avenue, that it became known as Bloody Corner. One Cleveland murder, which did not occur at that intersection, was the killing of Chuck O'Neil, a local booze baron, who was shot in the back as he sat in the window of his home. The interesting thing about this murder is that O'Neil at the time was supposedly in the county jail serving a thirty-day sentence. His murder somewhat embarrassed the prison authorities. Racketeers in Cleveland, as elsewhere, also began to move in on legitimate enterprises; they made a drive to take over the undertakers, during which at least one hearse was blown up.

Farther to the south, in Cincinnati, an energetic and elegant man named George Remus was among the earliest successful bootleggers; he owned seven distilleries in nearby Kentucky, and at one point he claimed to have paid $250,000 to a friend of the United States Attorney General to permit his operations to go undisturbed. Remus was a lawyer by profession; he quickly saw the opportunities in the prohibition law. First he bought his distilleries quite legally. Then they produced medicinal alcohol, also quite legally. But when the alcohol was shipped out of the distilleries, gangsters who were also organized by Remus stole it, and it went into illegal channels. This was a profitable business and Remus lived in luxurious fashion in a mansion on a suburban estate. During one of his parties he gave each of the ladies present, as a small keepsake, a Pontiac sedan.

At various times Remus served five jail sentences. While serving time in the Atlanta Penitentiary, he arranged for his cell to have maid service and fresh flowers each day. During one nineteen-month stretch, he began to get reports that his wife, Imogen, was being excessively friendly with another man — and to make things worse, the man was the federal agent who had gathered the evidence against

[48]

George Remus, titan of early bootleggers, shown behind bars during one of his five prison sentences for violation of liquor laws. As generous as he was rich, he often served guests $100 bills under their plates in his suburban mansion. (UPI Photo)

him. Just before Remus was released in 1927 she filed suit for divorce and he filed a countersuit. But shortly after he returned to Cincinnati he followed her into a city park and shot her in the stomach, killing her. He was tried and declared insane, but was quickly released from the asylum on a court writ. As time went on, the Remus mob also dominated the St. Louis bootlegging scene.

The gangster infection grew and flourished throughout America on illegal liquor money. It probably would have existed in lesser form on the proceeds of gambling and prostitution, but the flow of money for booze caused it to grow and spread. There were several reasons for this. The first was that a majority of Americans did not con-

Ingenious Americans found many ways to get around the liquor laws. Besides hollow canes and hip flasks, booze could be toted about in Russian boots, shown above. (Library of Congress)

sider alcoholic drink in itself wicked; therefore, it seemed to them that there was nothing wrong in continuing to drink it and to pay bootleggers for it. The second was that true enforcement of prohibition would cost a great deal of money. Wayne Wheeler at first predicted that it would take $5 million a year for the first several years and perhaps less thereafter; a few years later Prohibition Commissioner James M. Doran asked for $300 million to enforce the law — and received about $12 million. Doran was an earnest dry who wanted to do a good job. The trouble was that other drys either could not believe the extent of the bootlegging problem or were unable to admit it. If they agreed that a majority of United States citizens did not support the law, they would say in effect that it was a measure being imposed on all Americans by a dry minority, and this could only lead to its repeal. The third reason was an extension of the second. A law so widely disobeyed could be enforced only if there were an enormous number of police; a joke of the day said that real enforcement would require half of America to watch the other half. Bishop James Cannon, one of the leaders of the Anti-Saloon League, once suggested that the army should be called out to arrest liquor violators. But not even most drys really wanted a police state.

Further, the arrests that were made jammed the courts and crowded the prisons. In the first four years of prohibition, the number of inmates of federal prisons nearly doubled and the situation in many local jails was even worse. Two-thirds of the liquor-law violators brought into court pled guilty; in practice, this usually meant that they had arranged in advance with the prosecutor to get off with a small fine, thus keeping justice of a sort moving along. Roughly half of the time spent by federal attorneys throughout the country was devoted to liquor-law cases; in one district of Alabama that figure was 90 percent, and in the state of Kentucky it was 75 percent. The drys resisted any increase in the numbers of prisons, courts, or prosecuting attorneys for the same reasons they resisted any increase in the enforcement effort.

Occasional efforts were made to have true enforcement. In 1924, for example, Brigadier General Smedley D. Butler, a Marine Corps officer who had been a hero of World War I, was put on leave of absence at the request of the mayor of Philadelphia and was sworn in as director of public safety of that city. He organized the police admirably, and in five days they closed nearly six hundred speakeasies. In the first week they made two thousand arrests. But General Butler slowly began to realize that nothing happened to the people who had been arrested. The city judges turned them

[51]

Marine Corps General Smedley Butler, who tried to enforce prohibition in Philadelphia. (Photo by Cushing)

loose as fast as he brought them in — if other politicians didn't first intervene to keep them from even getting to court. Finally, after two years, the general went back to the Marine Corps. In that time he had arrested more than 6,000 people, but only 212 had been convicted. "Trying to enforce the law in Philadelphia," he later commented, "was worse than any battle I ever was in."

General Butler's experience spotlighted another evil. Prohibition, in addition to sustaining gangsters in most large cities, jamming the prisons, and clogging the judicial system, contributed to the widespread corruption of politicians and officials. The bosses and judges of Philadelphia who saw to it that arrested bootleggers were freed had their counterparts throughout the country. One anti-prohibition group screened *The New York Times* Index from

January 1, 1927, to October 1, 1928, and listed from it the many stories of prohibition corruption during that period. In Philadelphia, the list showed, a city magistrate was sentenced to six years in prison for accepting $87,993 in bribes involving prohibition cases over an eight-month period; perhaps General Butler felt better when he saw that. But the list also showed that throughout the country various city and state officials were indicted or convicted on similar charges. Certainly graft in high places was not unique to prohibition, but the combination of more money than was available in any other racket with laws that most people disliked made liquor-law bribery an easy thing both to give and to take.

The country seemed to be bogging down in prohibition lawlessness that the drys would not see; and the drys were in control. Foreigners considered the United States the most lawless country on earth. But certain basic conditions were beginning to change. Politically, the fight between the drys and the wets tended to be a fight between country and city. It had always been the rural churches that backed the Anti-Saloon League, and they were inclined to look upon themselves as protecting traditional American values against the immoral cities that were full of recently arrived immigrants. In its more extreme forms, this feeling led some prohibitionists to ally themselves with the Ku Klux Klan and to make statements not only against wets, but also against Catholics and first- or second-generation Americans. But, at the same time, the whole United States was becoming more urban. Radio and the movies were reaching into the smallest villages. Local newspapers were disappearing and city newspapers were gaining circulation in the surrounding countryside. People were moving from the country to the cities, and cities were becoming larger and spreading farther. The rural foundations of the dry cause were gradually crumbling away.

The St. Valentine's Day Massacre

Capone successfully maintained his position as the most powerful figure in the Chicago jungle, but at times he had to work to keep it. When smaller thugs tried to shake off his discipline they were summarily chopped down. And in April of 1927 there was an election for mayor of Chicago in which Al took part with some effect.

The incumbent mayor, William E. Dever, was an innocent man who had been elected on a reform ticket. He thought that he could control the city and enforce the prohibition law in it. Time had shown that he could not. But he continued to try, and his efforts were like mosquito bites to the gangsters, minor but irritating. They decided that they must have Big Bill Thompson, the mayor who had preceded Dever, back again. Big Bill was openly wet, made no effort to control the mobsters, and saved his anger for such immediate targets as the king of England, whom he once offered to punch in the nose, thus delighting his Irish supporters.

The tactics used to elect this buffoon were only a little more subtle than those Capone had used in Cicero a few years previously. For one thing, Al contributed something like $250,000 to the Thompson campaign. But he also dispatched his men to take more direct action. Vincent Drucci, now leading the O'Banion-Weiss mob, set out to kidnap an alderman of annoyingly liberal viewpoint and to wreck his office. Word of this planned attack reached the police, and Drucci and two of his crew were arrested before they could put it into action. No sooner were they brought to the police station than Drucci's lawyer was knocking at the door of the Criminal Court, asking for a writ of habeas corpus to free them. The police put them back in the car and wearily started off to court.

*Openly wet candidate "Big Bill" Thompson, aided by
a huge campaign contribution from Al Capone, was reelected mayor of Chicago by a landslide in 1927. (Photo by Cushing)*

Drucci was handcuffed to Police Detective Danny Healy. The
gangster was sure to go free in short order and his arrogance got
the best of him; he started to curse and berate Healy. The policeman
told him to shut up. In a rage, Drucci got up in the car on one leg,
turned, and hit Healy on the head with his free hand, at the same
time trying to take away his pistol. Healy shot him four times.
Drucci was delivered to the morgue, while his two companions
went on to the courtroom and their freedom.

[55]

Big Bill Thompson was reelected. Then Capone turned to some of his other problems. First among them were the Aiello brothers, nine Sicilians who had decided to remove Antonio Lombardo, the Capone man now at the head of the Unione Siciliana. Branches of that organization were in all the major cities, so the Aiellos dispatched friends to New York, Cleveland, Pittsburgh, St. Louis, and other cities to start a rebellion against Lombardo. The major results of this effort were that Capone had two Aiellos killed, and a number of dissident members of the Unione in St. Louis were shot. That took care of the rebellion.

The seven remaining Aiellos, however, continued to press their luck. They joined forces with Bugs Moran, a man with more brawn than brain who had succeeded the late Vincent Drucci as leader of the O'Banion gang. Secretly they decided to kill Al Capone. First, they made four attempts to have him shot by gunmen brought in from outside. The police were baffled, over a period of time, to find the bodies of four well-dressed crooks from New York, St. Louis (two of them), and Cleveland, each with considerable money in his pocket and each holding a nickel in his right hand — the contemptuous reward paid to an unskillful killer by a more adept one.

Then the Aiellos took another tack. They offered the cook of the Little Italy Café a bribe of $10,000 to poison Capone; the cook, however, notified Capone of the offer. Once a week for six weeks thereafter a member of the Aiello gang was found dead. Then the police, starting with information from an informer, uncovered a machine-gun nest set up overlooking the home of Antonio Lombardo. Material they found there led them to arrest Joseph Aiello and four others, one of them a gunman from Milwaukee who described another machine-gun trap, this one looking down on a cigar store that Capone visited regularly.

Aiello and the others were taken to the Detective Bureau. Not long after they arrived, one of the police officers saw a half dozen taxis pull up outside. Twenty-five men got out. Some moved off to stand in doorways along the street, some walked up and down the street. Others moved into the alley behind the bureau to watch the back door. Three men came up to the front door, one of them taking his pistol from its shoulder holster and sliding it into his side pocket as he came. It was the Capone gang, in search of Joseph Aiello.

A group of policemen soon collared the three at the front door, who turned out to be New York gunmen hired by Capone. At this show of police force, the other patrolling gangsters disappeared. The three hoodlums were put into a cell next to Aiello. Then an Italian-speaking policeman was quickly fitted out with old clothes and put into a cell across the corridor. He heard the New Yorkers telling Aiello in Sicilian dialect that he — Aiello — was dead; he wouldn't even get to the end of the street when the police released him. Aiello begged for mercy, but to no avail.

As it turned out, Joseph Aiello was not killed as he left the

Notorious gangland chieftain George ("Bugs") Moran. (UPI Photo)

Detective Bureau; the police escorted him to a taxi and he drove away and disappeared, hiding in an outlying area of the city. Although he continued to plot against Capone, he finally decided to quit and leave town. Carrying a ticket for Brownsville, Texas, he left his hiding place to enter a taxi. Two waiting machine gunners, on opposite sides of the street, filled him with fifty-nine bullets.

Meanwhile, Bugs Moran and his O'Banion gang had been giving moral support to the Aiellos, but not much else. They were moving toward disaster in another direction. Moran handled whiskey that Capone obtained through the Purple Gang of Detroit; the brand name was Old Log Cabin. Moran decided that he was being charged too much, and so he switched to a cheaper brand from another source, at the same time informing Capone that he was through with his brand. Al accepted this, and made arrangements to distribute his stuff through someone else. But Moran soon found that his customers much preferred Old Log Cabin and that they were switching to the new distributor of it. Bugs was not smart; he went back to Capone and said that he wanted to handle that brand again, only to be told that he couldn't have any — his competitors were now selling it.

Immediately thereafter, shipments of Old Log Cabin moving from Detroit to Chicago began to be hijacked with increasing frequency. At the same time Moran was somehow able to offer that brand again to his customers. Neither Capone nor the Purple Gang had any doubt as to what was happening, but they bided their time. Then a complete shipload of the whiskey arrived in Chicago and was promptly stolen. Capone and Company decided that enough was enough. They placed an agent in contact with Moran; this man over a period of time was able to provide Bugs with shipments of Capone whiskey that supposedly had been hijacked. Then he called Moran to say that the next day he would have a particularly large shipment; Moran said that he would buy it and told the caller to deliver it at his garage on North Clark Street, where his entire staff would be waiting.

The delivery day was February 14, 1929 — St. Valentine's Day. It was cold and windy. During the morning, what appeared to be a police car drew up outside the Moran garage, which masqueraded as the base of operations for a furniture-moving company. Out of the car stepped two men in police uniform and three in plain clothes; they walked over to the garage and entered the front door. Neighbors heard a chattering noise, then two reports that they assumed were caused by a backfiring truck in the garage. This drew

The innocent facade of the Moran garage, headquarters of Capone's enemies. Behind it, gangland's bloodiest killing took place — the St. Valentine's Day massacre. (Photo by Cushing)

several people to their windows in time to see two men in civilian clothes emerge from the garage with their hands up, followed by the apparent policemen carrying guns. The entire group climbed into the car and drove off.

Most of the onlookers assumed, as was intended, that this was some kind of a police raid. One woman, however, went out and tried the garage door, only to find it jammed shut. She called a man, who shoved the door open and went in; a moment later he came running back, crying that the garage was full of dead men.

The police arrived to find three bodies in a bloody line on the floor along one wall, a fourth crosswise at their feet, a fifth lying across a chair, and a sixth lying on the floor nearby. One man, Frank Gusenberg, was still alive though mortally wounded. All but one were members of the Moran gang; the exception was a young oculist, Dr. R. H. Schwimmer, who was a sentimental admirer of mobsters and liked to pal around with them. All had been machine-gunned. Two had also been blasted with shotguns — the "back-firing" sounds heard by the neighbors.

Moran himself was lucky. He and two of his men had been walking along the street just as the fake policemen went into the garage. They thought it was some sort of legitimate raid and quickly moved away. Next day, when he was questioned by the police, Moran blurted out, "Only the Capone gang kills like that," and then would say no more.

What evidently had happened was that two St. Louis killers, who were unknown in Chicago and could therefore pass as police-men, wore the uniforms. The others were Capone gangsters. While they waited in the entrance hall, the men in uniform went first and pretended to arrest the Moran crew, lining them up against the wall, facing it, in a normal procedure to search them. Moran's people did as they were told, expecting that they would merely have a trip to jail and a brief wait until their lawyers got them out. Instead, the gangsters then moved in from the hallway and shot them. One of the murdered men looked and dressed a little like Moran, and the execution squad probably thought that they had killed the boss himself.

Victims of the St. Valentine's Day massacre. (UPI Photo)

Changing Attitudes

Since the enactment of prohibition, the country had been going through the boom of the 1920's. The drys were quick to say that the money diverted from the purchase of booze was being used to buy consumer goods instead, and thus was the cause of the growing prosperity. Indeed, they said, if prosperity were to continue, prohibition had to remain in force. Throughout the history of prohibition many drys seem to have had an honest problem: they confused law with fact. If the law said the country was dry, it must be dry, and all the publicity to the contrary was merely the invention of news writers. The drys just could not believe that great amounts of money still were being spent on liquor — probably more than ever before.

But since the enactment of prohibition, the roles of the wets and drys had in many ways been reversed. The drys were now in control and therefore were on the defensive. Where previously every crime, every bribed policeman or judge, every drunkard was blamed by the drys on the saloon, now every one of those things was blamed not only by the wets, but by a growing number of other people, on prohibition. Ironically, the prohibition law also made the wets respectable, for no longer were they the distillers and brewers whose own business depended on the sale of alcholic drink. Instead they were responsible people who honestly thought prohibition was bad.

Congress also began to grow restive under the spurs of the Anti-Saloon League. Too many congressmen had been pushed too far and too often by the league, frequently against their better judgment. Members of Congress still voted dry, while in private they drank what they pleased — they still were scared of the league — but they no longer responded as quickly or as politely to the com-

[62]

mands issued by Wayne Wheeler. And Wheeler himself grew ill, finally dying in 1927, a few months after the simultaneous death of his wife by fire and his father-in-law by heart attack. As Andrew Sinclair, the British student of the prohibition era, commented on Wheeler, these tragedies "removed him from the unkind tongues of all except those Anti-Saloon League leaders who spoke at his funeral." His jealous successors were far more petty and less able men than he.

Prohibition had begun as a reform movement among people who felt that it would improve the human condition. Often these were the same people who fought for child labor laws, women's suffrage, and other similar reforms. But it is notable that during the actual period of prohibition, few other reforms took place. When the drys did suggest other reforms, they chose things that seemed even more repressive than prohibition. They seriously asked at various times that smoking, dancing, and jazz music be made illegal. As a result, many individuals were not only disillusioned with prohibition but also frightened of the possible results of any new reform.

Various ideas were put forth to modify the dry laws. The most frequent suggestion was to make beer and light wine legal; it might be possible to keep some prohibition and yet cut the ground out from under the criminals by giving the public something moderately alcoholic that they could drink legally. But the drys would have none of this. To most of them, alcohol itself was wicked; it was evil as it stood in the bottle. They did not greatly care about the practical matters of enforcement or whether more people might get drunk under one system than another. To them a law that legalized any form of alcoholic drink would legalize an evil; there could be no compromise with evil — and that was that.

In the presidential election of 1928, Alfred E. Smith, a New

York City Democrat, faced Herbert Hoover, a well-known Republican who had been wartime food administrator and had carried out other thankless government jobs with distinction. Smith, who represented the big-city vote, was wet, Hoover was dry; it was he who called prohibition "an experiment, noble in motive and far-reaching in purpose." As a result, the two major parties for the first time had to take firm positions on prohibition; the Democrats became the wets and the Republicans became the drys. Hoover won.

One of President Hoover's first acts was to appoint a commission to study law enforcement, with emphasis on the Eighteenth Amendment, and to make recommendations for its improvement. He had problems in assembling this commission, which had to be acceptable to the drys and at the same time to be composed of apparently moderate men who were not firmly committed to either side. As its head he appointed an attorney, George W. Wickersham. It is an indication of Hoover's difficulties in filling this post that Wickersham was the President's fourth choice.

Hoover was the first President to make a real effort to enforce prohibition. He set about building more prisons and insisted on stricter enforcement of the laws. The yearly number of arrests for prohibition violations tripled during Hoover's term, partly because he finally transferred the Prohibition Bureau to the Justice Department.

The Wickersham Commission came back with a report that Hoover did not expect; they had found that they could not study law enforcement without studying whether or not the Eighteenth Amendment could *be* enforced. A majority of the commissioners wanted either a major change in that amendment or complete repeal of it, and only one of the eleven commission members objected to sending the Eighteenth Amendment back to the country for another vote. A majority of them felt that enforcement would require measures that a democracy would not tolerate. But politics had to be served, and somehow all but one of the members were persuaded to sign what purported to be a summary of their findings. It opposed repeal and said that the dry laws should be enforced more strictly. This summary was what President Hoover released to Congress and the press.

Twenty-four hours later, however, the complete report was made public. The press immediately noted the difference between the summary and the body; reactions varied from loud guffaws to indignant editorials, and the New York *World* published a poem

A caricature of newspaper columnist Franklin P. Adams. FPA's short poem "Prohibition Is an Awful Flop" caught the spirit of the times, notably Americans' disenchantment with the Noble Experiment. (Photo by Cushing)

by Franklin P. Adams that neatly described the way most people now saw the findings of the Wickersham Commission:

> *Prohibition is an awful flop.*
> *   We like it.*
> *It can't stop what it's meant to stop.*
> *   We like it.*
> *It's left a trail of graft and slime,*
> *It don't prohibit worth a dime,*
> *It's filled our land with vice and crime,*
> *   Nevertheless, we're for it.*

The attempt to hide or twist the real meaning of the Wickersham report probably did as much to injure the dry cause as did the basic contents of the report itself.

The Reaction

One gangster supposedly called the St. Valentine's Day Massacre "lousy public relations." It certainly was. It was headlined throughout the country, and many people who had taken a romantic view of gangsters in the past began to think differently about them. People also began to wonder about their main source of money, bootlegging. In addition, the massacre led a number of people to decide that Chicago could do without Al Capone. Among these was a private group known as the Chicago Crime Commission; another body, this one anonymous, entitled The Citizens' Committee (and popularly called The Secret Six), stemmed from the Chicago Chamber of Commerce; and before long there was Herbert Hoover himself, represented by Treasury Department and Justice Department officers working with The Secret Six.

Meanwhile Frank Costello, the powerful New York gang leader who shunned publicity as much as Capone loved it, sent out a call for the criminal chiefs of the country to gather at Atlantic City to talk things over. Costello did not like the publicity that the massacre had drawn and he liked even less the way things were shaping up between the nation's gangs. Those outside Chicago were beginning to take sides in the Chicago battles, and it looked as though all of gangsterdom would soon be murdering each other. That, of course, would be very bad for business.

About fifty gang leaders came to the Atlantic City convention. They came from New York and Chicago naturally, and also from Philadelphia, Detroit, Cincinnati, Dayton, St. Louis, and Kansas City, as well as from smaller places. Costello, a thin, quiet man, contrasted severely with the plump, flashy, smiling Capone, but he made his point and Capone listened. There had to be peace among the gangs. The assemblage decided upon the areas in which each group would be supreme. Moreover, Costello saw to it that Capone and Moran sat down and made an agreement concerning the division of Chicago itself. They both signed it.

Capone and his bodyguard, Frank Rio, returning home to Chicago from Atlantic City, were to change trains at Philadelphia. To kill time between trains, they went to see a movie. On their way out of the theater they were recognized by police, stopped, and searched. Each of them had a pistol. Sixteen and a half hours afterward they were each sentenced to a year in prison for carrying concealed weapons. It was later suggested that Capone had planned this whole thing in order to get himself safely locked up and out

[67]

of the reach of Moran, but that seems doubtful. More likely, he had expected to receive little if any punishment — after all, he was The Big Fellow. He had not even bothered to call in the lawyers who might have freed him if they had started in time. But he was outside his own territory and he had no power with the Philadelphia authorities; here was one vicious criminal that they could safely punish. Like more and more Americans, Philadelphians did not consider Capone a hero.

Public disgust with prohibition and everything connected with it was building in many ways. A magazine called *Plain Talk*, in July of 1930, printed as its lead article a twenty-two-page report called "Ohio — Lawless and Unashamed." It described what was going on in the home state of the Anti-Saloon League. As an example, at the state convention of the Ohio League of Republican Clubs in Columbus, the state capital, on the preceding March 6, "The Honorable Edward Schorr, Director of the Ohio State Department of Commerce, warm personal friend and campaign backer of Governor Cooper, thoughtfully had caused a portable bar to be set up in a suite of rooms in the Deshler-Wallick Hotel where he acted as host while a corps of capable bartenders dispensed spiritous liquors to all comers from noon until 5:30 P.M." As a result, the keynote speaker that evening made a talk supporting prohibition to an audience most of whom had just been enjoying many free drinks.

In rural areas and small towns of Ohio, the magazine further pointed out, the enforcement of dry laws was in the hands of constables and justices of the peace whose income depended on the fines levied. As a result, almost anyone arrested was automatically found guilty and, "If the fee-grabbing constables could not find liquor they frequently framed victims. Whiskey bottles often were planted

[68]

in parked cars and later the innocent owners would be arrested and fined before what amounted to kangaroo courts."

This same kind of thing was going on in other states, of course. The reason that the magazine selected Ohio was because that state was nationally known as the home of the Anti-Saloon League, and therefore what went on there was most damaging to that organization.

As people began to recoil from prohibition, various groups sprang up to foster repeal. Most startling to the drys, who felt that womankind was automatically on their side, was the formation of the Women's Organization for National Prohibition Reform, led by Mrs. C. H. Sabin, who had been the first woman member of the Republican National Committee. Some of the prohibitionists failed

Portrait of Mrs. C. H. Sabin, of the Women's Organization for National Prohibition Reform. (Photo by Cushing)

to respond like gentlemen and lost votes by such intemperate comments as that of Dr. D. Leigh Colvin, who spoke of Mrs. Sabin's group as "wet women who, like the drunkards whom their program will produce, would take pennies off the eyes of the dead for the sake of legalizing booze."

The group that actually spearheaded the wet counterattack was the Association Against the Prohibition Amendment. It borrowed the tactics of the Anti-Saloon League and used them against it, supporting all wets in all elections, keeping records of politicians' votes, and pouring forth propaganda against prohibition. It was financed privately by rich men who had various motives, among them the hope that taxes on legal liquor could be substituted for corporation and income taxes. Very little of the association's money came from the liquor interests themselves. At the same time that this organization was growing, the money contributed to the Anti-Saloon League was dwindling.

The depression that began with the stock market crash of 1929 and slid perilously downward through the early 1930's was another blow at prohibition. When people were starving, the morals of prohibition seemed merely silly. With many people out of work it appeared scandalous that gangsters were still draining off whatever money people could afford to spend for drink; if prohibition was done away with, that money would go to support honest men. In a combination of propaganda and naïveté, some wets even announced that if alcoholic drink was made legal, the depression would end. The drys, who had claimed the boom years to be the result of prohibition, were hard put to fight back.

The public's changing attitude toward the Volstead Act, the bootleggers, and the gangster who provided the booze was well illustrated by the reception that greeted Al Capone when he got out of jail in Pennsylvania and returned to Chicago in 1930. No longer did Chicagoans look on him as The Big Fellow, an adventurer, a sort of modern Robin Hood who supplied the drink, gambling, and women that Chicago consumed. Now he was just a flashy crook. The Chicago Crime Commission labeled him Public Enemy Number One. In expectation of his arrival, the Chicago police assigned twenty-four men to guard his home and arrest him on sight. He went instead to the Hawthorne Restaurant, his Cicero headquarters, and from there he and his lawyer called on the Chicago police. There was no charge against him and no warrant; the police were reduced simply to asking him to leave town. This he would not do. Then the police assigned two men to follow him wherever he went and report on whatever he did. This was not the Chicago Al had known before. He left the Windy City and began traveling around the country, but wherever he went he was harassed by the police.

At the same time President Hoover, by means of Treasury and Justice agents, was closing in on him. When Capone returned to Chicago, he was arrested by federal agents for income tax evasion, and on October 18 was found guilty on five counts. He was fined $50,000, assessed $20,000 in costs, and sentenced to eleven years in prison. Just before the train left carrying him to the penitentiary he commented, "There was too much overhead in my business anyhow, paying off all the time and replacing trucks and breweries. They ought to make it legitimate."

Al was among the last people in the country to reach that conclusion. There were, however, a few notables who never really got to it. Henry Ford announced that if prohibition was repealed he would close his factories, upon which the *New Yorker* magazine commented, "It would be a great pity to have Detroit's two leading industries destroyed at one blow."

[71]

Repeal

The depression defeated the Republicans in the election of 1932. The Democrats in the preceding election had become identified as the wets, and therefore the depression in one sense led directly to prohibition's repeal. But by 1932 prohibition would probably have been repealed no matter who won. The Republican platform called for the resubmission of the Eighteenth Amendment to the states. Perhaps the Republicans would have attempted to keep a few more federal controls, and perhaps that would have been wise. Both sides, however, realized the depth of public feeling on the subject. When Franklin Delano Roosevelt accepted the Democratic nomination for

A pro-repeal "Beer for Prosperity" parade in New York City, 1932. (Photo by Cushing)

president, he announced in his acceptance speech, "I say to you that from this date on, the Eighteenth Amendment is doomed!" And the incumbent Hoover, three months before the election, said that the Eighteenth Amendment should be repealed; he surrounded his comment with so many hedges, however, that no one gave him much credit for it.

The lame duck Congress — the body voted out by the election but still sitting until new members are sworn in — also saw which way the hurricane was blowing. It did not leave the question for its successor, but resoundingly put through an overwhelming vote in both houses for a Twenty-First Amendment that would repeal the Eighteenth.

Now that the wets were riding high they were able to insist that the amendment be submitted to elected conventions in each state. These conventions were to be elected by straight numerical majorities. Since the passage of the Eighteenth Amendment, the trend of population had definitely changed; there now were more people living in cities than in rural areas. Yet state legislatures still had dominant representation from country districts. Generally cities voted wet, rural areas voted dry. By demanding the convention system, the wets ensured that the city vote would exercise its full strength.

When President Roosevelt took office he greatly cut the budgets of the prohibition enforcement agencies and at the same time asked Congress to modify the Volstead Act to permit the manufacture and sale of beer with an alcoholic content of 3.2 percent. Congress was eager to oblige; on April 7, 1933, the beer trucks rolled out again legally. On April 10 the first state convention was held in Michigan. Once again the states hustled to ratify a constitutional amendment, this one repealing the Eighteenth. Utah, the thirty-sixth state to vote for ratification, did so on December 5.

The Noble Experiment had ended. There were celebrations throughout the land, but the liquor that the celebrants drank was still bootleg — there had been no opportunity to put in supplies of legal stuff.

The Morning After

Prohibition, at first a liberal reform, became one of the greatest examples of conservative repression. How could this be? It was mainly because the reform was not workable. A strongly emotional minority was convinced that only through prohibition could the country be saved. This minority joined forces with skillful politicians to form the most powerful pressure group that America had seen to that time, the Anti-Saloon League. They built up a state of national fear about well-known evils. They drummed into the public consciousness that only their particular remedy could cure those evils. And so the measure was passed. It did not work, but the reformers could not admit that, partly because they were so committed emotionally that they could not believe that their cure-all was useless and partly because they did not care to be ridiculed as false prophets. They still maintained that their extreme solution was the only one. Most of the country soon decided that they were wrong, but through their highly developed political controls they were able to force their views on the people for more than thirteen years.

Just what *did* prohibition accomplish?

It raised the question of how far in a democracy the gov-

[74]

ernment can go to make crimes out of customs that are acceptable to most of the people.

Perhaps it also dried the country up a little, especially at first. Medical records show a decline in admissions for alcoholic diseases in the first few years of prohibition; this could mean that at that time it was difficult or unfashionable to drink, or it could mean that it was unfashionable for doctors to diagnose illnesses as being alcoholic. Whichever the case, however, the figures soon rose again. There is also some evidence that drinking by working-class Americans became less common during prohibition; one study suggested that it decreased by half. Laborers may have drunk less, but those who did drink were reduced to home brew and the cheaper bootleg stuff. At best this was a mixed blessing, and it is not surprising that most labor unions were strongly against prohibition.

Upon repeal, the word "saloon" disappeared from the American language. When the Noble Experiment was over, no bar was called a saloon; most people realized that it was the old saloon, with its numerous evils, that had first led to prohibition. Whether it came back to life under other names is a matter for debate. Certainly in most places there were no establishments really like the old saloons. Changing attitudes and customs of other sorts probably had as much to do with that as the Eighteenth Amendment did, but a fair case can be made for the argument that prohibition really did do away with the old-time saloon.

Prohibition certainly increased the number of middle-class drinkers. The speakeasy was basically a middle-class institution and it appealed to men and women who wanted to be fashionable and sophisticated. The American middle class was the richest in the world. At least during the boom years of the 1920's they had the money and the time to imitate the truly rich, and one way to do it

[75]

"The Fleet Comes In!" — *a photomontage from* Ballyhoo Magazine *celebrating the end of prohibition in 1933. (Photo by Cushing)*

was to follow their drinking habits — or what were assumed to be their drinking habits. There is no real way to tell, but it is likely that the total number of Americans who drank increased during the prohibition period. Drinking customs changed in other ways, too. Men carried hip flasks of liquor so that they would have it at

[76]

places and times it was not otherwise available; cocktails became popular because the fruit juice, sugar, and other ingredients in them helped to reduce the bite of raw booze; drunkenness became acceptable socially in groups that would not have tolerated it before.

Legally, prohibition created a host of problems just because it *was* an unworkable law. It produced criminals whom few people considered criminals. A majority of Americans dealt at least occasionally with bootleggers; in doing so, they could not feel that these men were much different from legitimate merchants. If bootlegging was not actually evil, then what was wrong with bribing a policeman so that he would not arrest the bootlegger? And if the bootlegger was arrested, would bribing a judge to let him off be such a serious offense? As a result of one bad law, public regard for all laws diminished.

Prohibition also created the gangster. Before prohibition there were bosses and there was crime. Criminal organizations were relatively small, however, and they lived mainly off the proceeds of gambling and prostitution. When to these already prohibited activities was added the much more widespread and popular one of providing drink, money came tumbling into underworld coffers. This tremendous new income built up the criminals at a time when all American activity was being mechanized. The telephone, the car and truck, and the submachine gun greatly helped such perverted geniuses as Torrio and Capone to consolidate their gangs. But to do this effectively required money: money to buy the modern tools, money to pay the criminal employees, money to pay off the police and the politicians, and above all the lure of money — much more money — waiting to be made. That money, of course, came from alcohol. Without it, criminals would certainly have followed the modern trend to consolidation, but they would still have been in a small business. With it they became gangsters, the big businessmen of crime.

Gangsters did not disappear with the end of prohibition. Instead, like vicious insects leaving a rotten tree that was cut down, they went looking for new rackets. They moved into businesses and labor unions that were too weak to fend them off. They took over industrial laundries and dry-cleaning chains as well as barbers', bartenders', and taxi-drivers' unions to serve as their bases for extortion and blackmail operations. They also went beyond that, investing their considerable money in perfectly legitimate businesses, as any other rich men might do. Then they sat back quietly as long as things went to their liking. When things went otherwise, the businesses blew up — sometimes literally — and the public was startled to read in headlines that gangsters had penetrated some outwardly legitimate industry. Of course the gangsters still control most gambling in America. The market for prostitution has diminished with changing social customs, but racketeers control the narcotics trade and they have developed usury — the lending of money at tremendous, and illegal, interest rates sometimes ranging up to 300 percent — into a fine art. Not only do they squeeze every last drop of money out of their victim, but if the unfortunate borrower is a person of any importance in business or government he is forced to do the racketeers' bidding in that area. Many of the smaller businesses taken over by criminals belonged initially to men who became indebted to them in this way.

The old city and state gangster organizations have been consolidated into larger and more efficient groups under the nationwide control of what is commonly known as the Mafia. This move began in 1931; about the time prohibition ended a national "Commission" was formed to coordinate gangland operations throughout the coun-

[78]

try, to arbitrate disputes between gangs, and at times to step in and set right a badly run local organization or to appoint a local leader. The Commission consists of nine to twelve members. Today, criminal chiefs tend to be conservative businessmen in their dress and manner, and the majority operate quietly. Only occasionally does a gang murder or a high-level gang meeting reach the news, and then we know that this heritage of prohibition is still with us.

Bibliography

Allsop, Kenneth. *The Bootleggers and Their Era*. Garden City, N.Y.: Doubleday & Company, Inc., 1961.

Asbury, Herbert. *The Great Illusion*. Garden City, N.Y.: Doubleday & Company, Inc., 1950.

Burnham, John C. "New Perspectives on the Prohibition 'Experiment' of the 1920's," *Journal of Social History*, II (1968–69).

Carse, Robert. *Rum Row*. New York: Rinehart & Company, Inc., 1959.

Chidsey, Donald B. *On and Off the Wagon*. New York: Cowles Book Company, Inc., 1969.

Cressey, Donald R. *Theft of the Nation*. New York: Harper & Row, 1969.

Kobler, John. *Capone: The Life and World of Al Capone*. New York: Putnam's Sons, 1971.

Krout, John A. *The Origins of Prohibition*. New York: Alfred A. Knopf, 1925.

Liggett, Walter W. "Ohio — Lawless and Unashamed," *Plain Talk*, July 1930.

Merz, Charles. *The Dry Decade*. New York: Doubleday, Doran & Company, Inc., 1931.

Sinclair, Andrew. *Prohibition, the Era of Excess*. Boston: Little, Brown and Company, 1962.

Steuart, Justin. *Wayne Wheeler, Dry Boss*. New York: Fleming H. Revell Company, 1928.

Sullivan, Mark. *Our Times*, VI. New York: Charles Scribner's Sons, 1946.

Taylor, Robert Lewis. *Vessel of Wrath: The Life and Times of Carry Nation*. New York: The New American Library, 1966.

Timberlake, James H. *Prohibition and the Progressive Movement*. Cambridge, Mass.: Harvard University Press, 1963.

Time-Life Books, Editors. *This Fabulous Century*, III, IV. New York: Time-Life Books, 1969.

Whitlock, Brand. *The Little Green Shutter*. New York: D. Appleton and Company, 1931.

Wilbur, Ray Lyman, and Hyde, Arthur Mastick. *The Hoover Policies*. New York: Charles Scribner's Sons, 1937.

Index

[83]

Tommy gun. *See* Thompson submachine gun
Torrio, John, 25, 26, 32-39

Unione Siciliana. *See* Italo-American
National Union

Volstead Act, 15-16, 73
failure of enforcement, 50-53
provisions, 18, 21, 25, 28
Volstead, Andrew J., 15

WCTU. *See* Women's Christian Tem-
perance Union
Weiss, Hymie (Hyman), 39, 41, 46, 47
Wets and drys, 7

Wheeler, Wayne B., 10-15 18-19, 30-31,
50, 63
Whiskey
during prohibition, 26-28
Wickersham Commission, 64-66
Wilson, Woodrow, 13, 16
Women
drinking customs, 22-23
in the prohibition movement, 4-5
Women's Christian Temperance Union,
4, 5, 22
Women's Organization for National
Prohibition Reform, 69, 70
Wood alcohol, 16, 25
World War I
prohibition during, 13-14

James P. Barry has written a number of books and articles on historical subjects, including two others in the Focus Books series. He has also done both the photography and writing for a picture book on the Great Lakes that is to be published soon.

A 1940 graduate of Ohio State University (cum laude, with distinction, Phi Beta Kappa), he entered the army in that same year as a lieutenant of artillery. He served in the European theater of operations during World War II, then remained in the army for over twenty-five years, finally leaving it as a colonel. During that time he served in many places in the United States (including a tour in the Pentagon as senior editor for the Director of Army Intelligence) and abroad (including a tour as adviser to the Turkish army).

For several years he was a university administrator. He is now associated with an educational book publisher. Mr. Barry is a resident of Columbus, Ohio, and is married; his wife is a high-school librarian.